STOP WAIT GO

STOP WAIT GO

Rules for a Busy Mind

By Aruna Krishnan

COPYRIGHT © 2019 By Aruna Krishnan

All Rights Reserved. This book or any portion thereof may not be reproduced or used in any manner whatsoever without the express written permission of the publisher except for the use of brief quotations in a book review.

This book is dedicated to my Dad who is my biggest supporter and fan.

Listening to and understanding our inner sufferings will resolve most of the problems we encounter.

-Thich Nhat Hanh

CONTENTS

SECTION 1 - TRAFFIC LIGHTS

Chapter 1 - Purpose Of Traffic Lights   3

Chapter 2 - Red, Yellow, Green   9

SECTION 2 - WE ARE WHAT WE THINK

Chapter 3 - Input, Process, Output   15

Chapter 4 - Traffic Lights For Our Mind   19

SECTION 3 - THE 3-STEP PROCESS

Chapter 5 - Process Overview   27

SECTION 4 - STOP

Chapter 6 - Annabel - The Dedicated Friend   33

Chapter 7 - John - The Ambitious Employee   37

Chapter 8 - Sarah - The Doting Mother   41

Chapter 9 - Julia - The Dedicated Wife   45

SECTION 5 - WAIT

Chapter 10 - Annabel	51
Chapter 11 - John	55
Chapter 12 - Sarah	59
Chapter 13 - Julia	61

SECTION 6 - GO

Chapter 14 - Annabel	65
Chapter 15 - John	67
Chapter 16 - Sarah	69
Chapter 17 - Julia	71

Epilogue	73
The Dos And Don'ts Of Stress Management	75
Acknowledgements	79

STOP WAIT GO

Journal	81

PREFACE

As human beings we are programmed, by nature, to follow our instincts. Instinct helps us survive. It guides us away from dangerous situations. It helps us protect and provide for our families.

We often use this programming as an excuse to make decisions that are merely reactive. Concepts such as "Mindfulness" and "Emotional Intelligence" drive home the point of being empathetic. They show us how to be in control of our mind and actions. Both of them start with us basically recognizing our thoughts and feelings.

At one point in my life I wanted to redefine myself. I no longer wanted peoples' behavior to get the better of me. I had to start recognizing my self-worth. I needed to pinpoint what really mattered to me. My ultimate goal was to be happier. During my research process I found some recurring key principles that all pointed back to the theory that happiness is governed by our own thoughts. I applied that strategy to my life and soon realized wasteful thoughts and ill-feelings I'd been harboring towards certain individuals slowly disappeared. This convinced me I was doing something that made total sense.

Sometimes, even after I embraced a new way of thinking, I regressed into the old ways. But those times were only temporary glitches because by then I knew the best way to approach problems and achieve results. Getting back on track was easy.

This book uses the analogy of traffic lights to help explain how we can manage situations better by being more mindful and intentional with our actions and reactions.

SECTION 1
TRAFFIC LIGHTS

Why do we need traffic lights? What do they mean?

This section delves into the purpose and significance of traffic lights. It shows us how each element of the traffic light plays an important role in ensuring the safety of everyone present at the intersection.

Chapter 1

PURPOSE OF TRAFFIC LIGHTS

Have you ever wondered what would happen on a busy street if there were no traffic lights?

If we defined the traffic pecking order from highest to lowest the list would be: truck, car, motorcycle, bike, pedestrian. Due to its size, the truck would probably have the least to lose without the regulation of traffic lights. Yet, the truck would probably create the most havoc and damage.

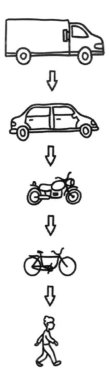

Let's assume the perspective of a person driving a car.

You're at the busy, and dreaded, intersection. Your first instinct is to avoid it at all costs, but you know there is no other choice but to get through it. Inevitably, your heart rate shoots up. Your cortisol levels rise and a stream of colorful words come out of your mouth as a way to cope with the stress. You don't want to take risks that will put you in danger. Neither do you want to be at fault for injuring a biker or a pedestrian. You want to avoid the drama, yet you really don't have a choice but to participate.

PURPOSE OF TRAFFIC LIGHTS 5

Now imagine in this same scenario that you are a student biking to school. Cars are zipping by, motorbikes are maneuvering their way around and people are making a dash across the street when they see the tiniest sign of a clearing. How are you going to get past all that chaos? Coming to a standstill may never get you to school on time. Taking your chances and charging through the mess puts you at risk of getting hit and injuring yourself.

Finally, the person at the bottom of the pecking order - the pedestrian - has to worry about trucks, cars, motorcycles and bicycles. What a burden! This is no different than the creature at the bottom of the food chain.

So how do traffic lights minimize the chaos? For starters, they create some basic rules that can be easily understood by both motorists and pedestrians.

Additionally, the lights:

- Set a cadence that regulates the flow for everyone involved
- Set expectations and create a habit for all those involved in traversing the street
- Take the chaos out of the equation and encourage more rational behavior

Without traffic lights, intersections would be a disaster.

PURPOSE OF TRAFFIC LIGHTS 7

Chapter 2

RED, YELLOW, GREEN

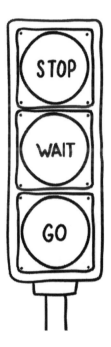

Red

Red in the context of traffic means "STOP!" It is considered the universal symbol for "Danger". It tends to be a subliminal signal that makes us break out from the constant movement and noise. It creates a moment to be courteous to others in the intersection. It is the primary means of facilitating the harmony needed on a busy street.

The red light, as annoying as it is at times, actually provides the sanity we need during our daily commutes. It gives us a chance to relax, watch the other cars go by, and observe people interact with one another.

Admittedly, on days when we are in a hurry, there can be nothing more aggravating than consecutive red lights. If you think about it though, those red lights probably prevent us from driving like a lunatic.

What if we were to ignore the red light? What would be some of the consequences? Crashes, injuries, damage all around, and so much more. It makes sense to take that pause and then correct. If the small interval of time during a red light can prevent casualties, why wouldn't we adhere to the rule?

Yellow

Yellow is usually the color associated with a warning.

It is not an absolute call out of a dangerous situation, but does indicate the need to be cautious and alert and that things are not in a state of "All Clear". The color yellow heightens our senses and challenges our presumption that we are in a good position to proceed as normal. It makes us "WAIT" for a brief second before making the next move.

Much like the consequences of ignoring the Red light, not acting in accordance with the Yellow light will result in damage and destruction. Warnings are made to shake up people's existing beliefs and draw their attention to different possibilities and outcomes. Seeing a yellow light should make people slow down enough to evaluate their current actions and determine if they should continue or stop. That decision could make a huge difference and reduce stress generated in traffic situations.

Green

We're all familiar with that feeling of knowing the light is about to turn green. It's liberating, isn't it? We feel as though we have earned it; especially if we have been waiting for the shift from red to green. We feel both the entitlement to proceed and the confidence that we have the right of way. It is reassurance that we are good to "GO".

In most cases at a green light we simply do a quick evaluation of trailing cars and then proceed in the direction of our destination. Being present and aware of our surroundings increases our ability to respond to traffic as needed.

SECTION 2
WE ARE WHAT WE THINK

Why do we react the way we do? How can we have some control over our thoughts?

This section provides some insight into these questions by using examples and analogies to show how our mind works. That knowledge helps us understand when corrective action is needed.

Chapter 3

INPUT, PROCESS, OUTPUT

The universal way to depict a flow of information includes three key elements as shown below.

This model can be used to show how the output is highly influenced by the inputs that go into the process. Let's look at a simple example of the food we eat. As the saying goes, "We are what we eat."

If we choose to consume nutritious food, our body processes it and gives us more favorable results. We feel good and are generally healthier.

INPUT = Good Food
PROCESS = Consumption and Digestion
OUTPUT = Healthy Lifestyle

On the flipside, if we primarily eat junk food, the end result is bad health and a harmful lifestyle.

INPUT = Junk Food
PROCESS = Consumption and Digestion
OUTPUT = Harmful Lifestyle

The interesting thing is that no matter what path you're on, the more you adhere to it, the more instinctual and natural it becomes.

The healthy eaters see the benefits to their body and their mood and continue to follow that path.

The not-so-healthy eaters care more about the immediate satisfaction that comes after eating a burger with fries. They repeatedly go back for more because it makes them feel good. Their taste buds grow accustomed to the flavor and therefore they crave it.

Two different perspectives, but both are ultimately influenced by the initial input and result in a respective outcome.

The Input-Process-Output flow is also applicable to how we think and therefore how we act. Let's look at an example from the earliest point in the human life cycle.

Babies learn (with experience) that by crying, they are sure to get attention. They learn this within the first few minutes of life. Sometimes the cry is genuine and is an expression of discomfort or need. At other times it is a definite way of attracting attention since they have learned this is one way to do so.

INPUT = Parent's response to baby's cries
PROCESS = Establishment of Cause-and-Effect
OUTPUT = Attention-seeking strategy

If parents don't respond to the baby's cry, such as when they are training them to sleep separately, the baby would soon understand that their cries are going to be in vain. Eventually, the baby gives up and goes to sleep. Here again, the input is the parents' response, or lack thereof, to the baby's cry. The output is the baby giving up the charade and going to sleep.

INPUT = Parent's non-responsiveness to baby's cry
PROCESS = Updated understanding of Cause-and-Effect
OUTPUT = Submission (to idea of sleeping separately)

This simply goes to prove that we are influenced by our surroundings.

Our experiences influence our thoughts, which influence our actions, which influence our habits.

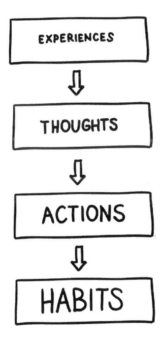

As we rinse and repeat through this cycle, those habits get ingrained and start to define our personalities. This really tells us that we have to be our own "thought police". We can choose how to process certain inputs and thereby determine the resultant outcome. We owe it to ourselves to do that.

For our safety. For our happiness.

Chapter 4

TRAFFIC LIGHTS FOR OUR MIND

We are faced with numerous situations and decisions in life. These can easily be equated to a busy intersection where there are crazy drivers, careless pedestrians and noisy distractions all at once.

We can add traffic lights to our thinking to help ease this pain. It is as simple as "STOP-WAIT-GO".

When we initially start to train our mind to apply the traffic lights, STOP is the most critical element. This is because when our mind is racing, we have gone beyond the possibility of reason. In order to reduce that irrationality, we must decide to take ourselves out of that situation.

After stopping, we need time to reason. This is also known as the WAIT phase. Although it may not always feel like we can be objective in matters of the heart, just taking that step back helps us think beyond ourselves.

Once we have had time to reason, we are ready to "GO" with a plan of action.

The next three examples create an analogy between driving on a freeway and how our mind works. The examples show us how to recognize the cues needed to "Stop", "Wait" or "Go".

MIND YOUR SPEED

Imagine you are driving on a freeway with a posted speed limit of 70 mph. How do you feel when you go 10 mph over the speed limit? What about 20 mph over? When you drive at 90 mph, do you still feel as though you are in control?

If an unexpected traffic condition occurred, could you respond to it effectively? Or are you taking the risk of having to veer off the road to avoid a potential accident? Would your response be more calculated, appropriate and timely if you were abiding by the speed limit?

This scenario can be equated to how we feel when we are extremely angry. Our mind is well over the normal speed limit. We are no longer in control of our thoughts. We tend to respond without any evaluation of the potential risks of those actions.

This type of behavior is commonly referred to as "Impulsive". The expression "Think Before You Act" was probably coined as a result of this type of reactiveness. It is always followed by a sense of regret and realization that you could have made a better decision. When we find ourselves in this mode, we have to "STOP".

Recognizing this cue is critical. It sets us up well to manage stress.

AVOID HIGHWAY HYPNOSIS

Do you know that feeling when you are driving in autopilot mode under "Highway Hypnosis"? Your brain knows the destination and you really don't have to do much thinking. Although we can operate safely in that mode to some extent, when we are not fully conscious of ourselves and our surroundings, we are at risk. Our reflexes are not as sharp, so we may not respond as quickly as needed to certain mishaps on the road.

This is an indication that we should pull over, refresh our mind, get back on track safely, and snap out of "Highway Hypnosis."

Likewise, in life, we are accustomed to reacting to certain situations in specific ways. For example, if someone yells at us we may choose to yell back because that is our defense mechanism. Others may choose instead to shut down and internalize their feelings.

Both of those reactions are habits developed over the years and, as a result, they become our go-to reactions. Neither of the responses above are healthy options in the long run.

So how do we break out of that cycle (assuming there is no imminent danger)? Simple...by pausing.

A mere pause helps us evaluate why that person might be yelling. It might be because they are having a bad day and you, unfortunately, got caught in the cross-fire. It might be a disguised cry for help. Either way, it is a great opportunity for us to be more kind and empathetic. But that is only possible with an initial pause to get our mind out of the "Why Me?" mode.

SET IT TO CRUISE

Every modern car today has "Cruise Control" functionality. Some cars even drive themselves! In both of these cases, the person behind the wheel has to make some sensible judgments on when to utilize those features.

Whether or not you choose to engage either of those features depends on your assessment of the surrounding traffic, the speed limit, the number of turns required and other such factors. The driver needs to ensure that the road conditions are safe and appropriate enough to go into "Cruise" mode. The lack of evaluation prior to doing this can be disastrous.

When can we set our actions to run in "Cruise Control" mode?

The repeated application of STOP-WAIT-GO to our thinking makes our decision-making process increasingly easier. When the process feels more instinctive and instantaneous, in essence, you are in "Cruise" mode.

SECTION 3
THE 3-STEP PROCESS

How can you train your mind to slow down and therefore increase your self-awareness?

This section lays out a process with intermediate decision points to easily determine how to navigate each step from STOP to WAIT to GO. The more we work through this process, the easier it becomes. Transitions between steps become quick, smooth and seamless.

Chapter 5

PROCESS OVERVIEW

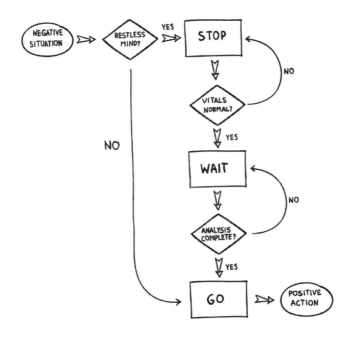

NEGATIVE SITUATION

When faced with a "Negative" situation, the first thing to focus on and understand is your state of mind (which determines the risk of overreacting).

If calm and collected, you can safely proceed to the decision making and action phase i.e. GO.

On the other hand, if you're feeling restless and agitated, then walk through the 3-step STOP-WAIT-GO process.

STOP

This is the most challenging step in the process. From personal experience and observation, the key to mastering this skill is practice. It takes a lot of willpower and self-discipline. It requires being open to a new way of thinking.

I was able to adopt this process after accepting the fact that we create our own stress. Whether it is a situation or a person "causing" our stress, we have to remember that we can choose how to respond when faced with those circumstances.

By "stopping", we allow ourselves to have some space. That space gives us a chance to drop our defenses and just be. It helps us get to our baseline mood and vitals which in turn puts us in the right frame of mind for the "WAIT" stage.

We cannot proceed to the "WAIT" stage until we have calmed down. Proceeding without this prerequisite would only result in a poor and incomplete execution of that phase.

WAIT

This step is where most of the analysis occurs. These are some of the questions we can ask ourselves:

- Have you identified the possible causes of stress?
- Have you considered the other person's point of view?
- Have you put this in the context of the bigger picture?
- Have you identified possible solutions?

Once we have cycled through these questions in earnest, we are likely to have a plan of action that is less erratic. It will likely be logical, kind or even considerate. Being able to look at things from a 15,000-foot viewpoint usually reveals that things are not as bad as we make them out to be.

The biggest factor in making this step successful is our willingness to consider someone else's angle. In most cases, we don't care enough to do that - we just vilify them if they trouble us. This basically makes us blame them for everything, and we just sit there feeling annoyed.

We certainly can't make them change how they behave, but we can change how we think or respond. So why wouldn't we? I am not saying we always have to give in or compromise. Instead, we should consider whether there is a need for empathy on our part. If the problem goes beyond showing empathy, we can either have a direct conversation with them, get help to solve the conflict or, worst case, part ways.

Once we have formulated an action plan, we can move on to the "GO" phase.

GO

At this point, all the hard work has been completed. We have taken the time to evaluate our problems and the root causes. We have also broadly outlined a potential solution. Whether the problem was relationship-based or situation-based, we are in a position to tackle it. Because we have gone through the 3-step process, we are able to move forward with genuinely good intentions.

Once we have become experts at applying the three-step process, the cycle time between initial "Negative" thought to "GO" becomes significantly less.

POSITIVE ACTION

By using this model, our actions are well thought out and have a tone of "positivity". This, therefore, increases the odds of receiving a positive response in return.

How can we apply this theory to practical situations? The next section conceptualizes this model with life-like scenarios.

SECTION 4
STOP

Were there instances in your life where you could have applied the 3-step process for a better outcome?

This section introduces four characters that encounter a difficult situation. The characters are fictional, but the scenarios are based on true events.

Each person has a different role and a different perspective, but the core problem for each of them is the same. Their thoughts become as chaotic as a busy intersection. This means they need to learn to regulate the flow of those thoughts in order to move forward safely.

The first step for each of them is to recognize when to "STOP".

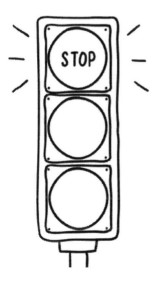

Chapter 6

ANNABEL - The Dedicated Friend

Let's look into the story of Annabel, a caring and reliable person. She embodies the perfect characteristics of a dedicated friend. She has a handful of close friends and always makes sure her interactions with them bring her true qualities to the table whether that means supporting them in times of doubt, sharing their happiness in times of success, or just being a friend without expectations. In other words, Annabel is the kind of friend we all seek and, unfortunately, rarely find.

Annabel was going about her day when she got a text from her friend Kim:

Kim: Hey girl! Plans this Saturday?
Annabel: Housework and errands. Nothing too fancy :) Why?
Kim: A few of the girls want to go to the new night club downtown - r u in?
Annabel: Hmm...I have to take the kids for swim class on Sunday morning. I'll pass.
Kim: Come on girl...It's been so long. It'll be fun.

Annabel hadn't met with her friends for a few months, so after pondering for a few minutes she replied:

Annabel: OK :) What time?
Kim: I'll pick you up at 7 PM.
Annabel: Cool! c u Saturday.

Annabel started to get excited about the girls night out. The anticipation got her through the work week. On Saturday morning, she woke up feeling energized. She did all her weekend errands with extra enthusiasm. She couldn't wait to unwind and just relax with her friends.

After making dinner she showered and picked out her best "little black dress" and jewelry. She finished up her look with a little makeup.

She had not heard from Kim since the original invite. It was about 7 PM. She called Kim, but the call went to voicemail. She left Kim a voicemail:

Annabel: Hey Kim, I'm all set. Let me know when you expect to be here.

Twenty minutes went by and Kim didn't call back. Annabel started getting worried. She called Kim's number again but got voicemail. She decided to call Kim's husband, Alex, just to make sure her friend was safe:

Annabel: Hi Alex, it's Annabel. Do you know where Kim is? She was going to meet me today at seven. I tried to call her, but it keeps going to voicemail.
Alex: Oh hey Annabel. Kim's right here. Here you go.
Kim: OH HEY Annabel. What up girl?

Annabel was a little agitated because she could tell Kim had consumed one too many drinks.

At this point we can see that Annabel is starting to have negative thoughts as a result of Kim's behavior. Her frustration stems from Kim not keeping her word. Annabel was caught up with the idea of having a night out, so now she is experiencing the initial symptoms of disappointment.

Annabel: Hi Kim. I was just calling because of the plan we talked about earlier this week. I am guessing those plans are off?

Annabel was resisting the urge to be sarcastic. She could feel herself getting very annoyed at this point.

Kim: Oh shoot Annabel! I completely forgot. Dang. Our neighbor offered to watch the kids and I jumped at the chance to have a night out with Alex. You understand right?

Annabel: What about the other girls?

Kim: Oh they are lame. They sent me a group text this morning requesting a raincheck. I guess they all had other plans. I should have told you that.

Annabel: Oh ok.

Kim: So sorry. I owe you one. Let's plan something soon.

Annabel: Ok Kim. Have a good night.

Annabel hung up quickly. She was outright angry. "What the heck??" she exclaimed. "This is freaking ridiculous!" She was mad that Kim hadn't thought to call her when the plans changed. She just couldn't digest Kim's lack of courtesy. Her mind swirled with a lot of negative thoughts.

It is at this point, given the situation, Annabel should quickly say to herself "STOP!" Ideally, that should happen before all the swirling. If it doesn't, then the next best thing would be to stop immediately after the recognition of those chaotic thoughts.

Learning how to recognize the onset of negative thoughts helps us prevent damage to ourselves. Something to realize is that negative thoughts, words or emotions towards someone else have to go through our bodies before they reach the other person. That means that we are in fact hurting ourselves more than we are the other person.

Chapter 7

JOHN - The Ambitious Employee

Our next character is John. John is a person who always brings his best to the workplace. He never looks at his job as "just a job". He is constantly thinking about how to do things better, how to bring more value to the company, and how the company could add more value to its customers. So all in all, John is a fully engaged employee.

John has worked in his firm for about two years as a Senior Business Consultant. He brings a lot of positive changes to his team by constructing new ways of solving problems and putting some structure in place to execute on those problems. The changes he implements results in his team delivering higher quality products with significantly fewer defects or customer complaints.

John's manager and his peers constantly acknowledge the difference John has made, and some of his peers look up to him as a mentor. His initiative and drive are visible to other teams and leaders in the company.

When it was time for year-end reviews, John went to meet his manager, Joe, with full confidence that he would get a promotion.

Joe: Good Morning, John!
John: Good Morning, Joe.
Joe: How've you been?
John: Good. Things have been going really well.
Joe: Yeah. I've heard a lot of positive feedback from your peers. I even got some feedback directly from a few customers. Great job!

John: Thanks, Joe.

John started to feel even more certain about the prospect of a promotion.

Joe: Ok. Let's get to it. As you know, every team is limited to a certain amount of bonuses and promotions. The reality is that we can't promote everyone on the team just because we think they did a more than decent job, you know?

John was a little perplexed by Joe's message.

Joe: Looking specifically at the goals you set at the beginning of the year, it seems you have been successful in meeting them. Kudos to you on that! You've been a great addition to the team. Your attitude has had a positive influence on the team.

John couldn't help thinking that this was going to be followed by a "BUT..."

Joe: From an individual perspective, I think you've excelled in your role. I want you to continue that passion going forward. Ideally, I would have recommended you for a promotion, but a few people on the team have taken some time to get up to speed after years of persisting. Those people are finally ready for their first promotion.

John couldn't believe what he was hearing.

Joe: I urge you to maintain your performance level so we can consider you for a promotion next year. Again, thank you for your efforts and I am so glad to have you on my team.

John was irritated.

Here, John feels he is being patronized. His ego is getting the better of him. He feels entitled to the promotion and is taking Joe's decision as an insult.

John: I feel I have made visible changes for both the team and the company. I am not sure why that is not being recognized and rewarded accordingly.

Joe: You have made a difference, John. But again, as I mentioned, there are two others who are finally making progress and deserve to get that recognition. You are already a high performer.

John was dumbstruck. He was so angry.

John: Ok, thank you, Joe.

John got up and left. He was afraid if he stayed it would get very ugly. The ugliness did remain in his head though. He did not understand Joe's logic. He felt he was robbed of recognition. He questioned why he tried so hard. He wondered why he cared so much. He felt both rejected and dejected.

Clearly, it is time for John to say "STOP!"

Once John gets to the point where he takes things personally, it becomes harder to be more objective. Applying the concept of "Emotional Intelligence", John needs to take control of himself and get back to a state of calm.

Chapter 8

SARAH - The Doting Mother

Now, let's meet Sarah. She has what is called a "Type-A" personality. She is very particular about keeping things organized and likes to take the lead in situations. She feels more comfortable when she is in "control".

When Sarah was younger, she did not tolerate boyfriends who were slobs or just plain lazy. She couldn't even fathom how people could be that way. She was definitely judgmental towards them.

Sarah eventually met the man she would marry. Although he was not a "Type-A", he also liked a certain level of order in his life. They got married and had two kids. They were both exceptional parents who stayed involved in all school activities and had their kids enrolled in plenty of extra-curricular activities.

The years went by with everything going according to plan...Sarah's plan for the most part. She was a great, loving mother and would do anything and everything for her kids. Her life was dedicated to raising these kids and they were always her number one priority. But when her son Kyle turned thirteen, she was faced with her first true parenting challenge.

Kyle was playing video games one morning but Sarah wanted him to stop and be "more productive".

Sarah: Kyle, what are you doing?
Kyle: I am playing video games.
Sarah: Don't you have homework to finish up?

Kyle: Yeah. I will do it after I finish this game.

Sarah: It's Sunday. I want you to finish up your breakfast and get your homework done.

Kyle: Mom, can you just stop?!

Sarah did not appreciate Kyle's tone.

We tend to reflect others' behavior towards us. When we get negative energy thrown our way we automatically want to respond back with the same tone. Our built-in "Fight or Flight" instinct causes that knee-jerk reaction to lash back, as Sarah starts to do with Kyle.

Sarah: Stop what? Asking you to be responsible and do your homework instead of goofing around?!

Kyle: Oh my gosh, Mom. Why are you always such a "Control Freak"? I said I would do my homework after this game, all right?

Sarah couldn't believe the push back she was getting. She couldn't understand how Kyle would even think this was appropriate behavior.

Sarah: Kyle! First of all, you cannot talk to me like that! Secondly, it is my job as a parent to keep you on track.

Kyle: Mom! I said I would finish this game and go and do my homework. Can you please just leave me alone?

Sarah couldn't believe the attitude she was getting, and it made her very angry.

Sarah: No, I cannot leave you alone. I need you to focus on your school work.

Kyle: Mom. Have you seen my grades lately?

Sarah: Excuse me? Am I the parent or are you?

Kyle: Seriously, Mom? You need to relax.

Sarah was no longer in control of herself. She set Kyle's breakfast down, walked up to the video game's power button and turned it off.

Sarah: You are grounded! Go to your room and work on your homework. No more video games for two weeks.

Kyle mumbled a few things and stormed off to his room. He banged his door shut.

On one hand, Sarah felt she had done the right thing. On the other hand, she felt she could have handled the situation with a little less emotion. She was left with a feeling of emptiness and helplessness. She wished she had "STOPPED" before she got carried away with enforcing her own agenda. She wanted to spend some time understanding how she could have handled the situation in a way that would have resulted in a win-win outcome. She loved her son and it hurt her that he was upset.

This shows us that in a situation of conflict, reflecting each other's negativity does not solve the problem. In fact, it creates a tremendous amount of stress and tension. It also, as we see in Sarah's case, causes regret. This regret, if channeled correctly, can help rectify the situation. Acknowledging and owning our mistake is the first step to correcting the way we think through and solve problems.

Chapter 9

JULIA - The Dedicated Wife

Our final character is Julia. She is a loving and caring person. As the oldest of four children, she learned to nurture at a very young age.

She is married to her husband, Josh. She cares for him deeply. She genuinely wants to see him happy. If he has a bad day, she talks him through it. If he is stressed out about anything, she calms him down. She really enjoys being his wife. His presence alone makes her happy. He is her best friend.

On their fifth anniversary, Julia was planning to surprise Josh with an intimate candlelight dinner. She was going to tell him some big news. She was pregnant! She was so excited.

She kissed him goodbye as he left for the day and reminded him to come home by 6:00 PM. Later that day Josh called Julia:

Josh: Hi Honey. Brandon, my friend from college is in town and wants to meet me this evening.
Julia: Ok Hon. But you remember it is our anniversary today, right?
Josh: Yeah Sweetie. We'll just have a couple of drinks and catch up. I'll be home by seven o'clock.
Julia: Seriously? Why can't you meet him tomorrow?
Josh: He is only in town for the day.

Julia was annoyed.

Julia: This sucks!
Josh: Babe, I promise, I'll be home in time to celebrate.
Julia: Ok...seven o'clock at the latest. OK??
Josh: Ok Honey. Love you.

Julia prepared everything for the evening. She cleaned and decorated the house. She made a delicious dinner. She freshened up and wore an elegant dress for the "date".

At 7:00 PM, Josh called her:

Josh: Hey, I am running a little late. Brandon only showed up thirty minutes ago. I'll leave for home by eight.
Julia: But honey, I am waiting for you so we can eat together.
Josh: I know. I promise I'll be there soon. Love you.
Julia: But...

Josh hung up before she could finish. This drove Julia crazy. She was really upset. A flurry of thoughts ran through her head:

Why was some idiot called Brandon more important to Josh?

It was their anniversary for goodness sake!

Why would Josh think eight o'clock was acceptable?

I do so much for him...why couldn't he do this small thing for me?

I deserve better.

She was on the verge of crying. She felt very lonely. She questioned if Josh truly loved her.

The moment we start to feel sorry for ourselves, and play the role of a "victim", we forget about how much inner strength we actually possess. It is so easy to fall into that trap. Pointing the finger at someone else gives us an excuse to not take responsibility for the situation. By expecting others to "fix their faults", we miss the angle of compassion. We don't consider their side of the story.

Julia had to "STOP" before she got too carried away with the "Why Me?" line of thinking.

SECTION 5
WAIT

Were you able to relate to the stories above? Have you been faced with similar situations?

In many cases, these situations can even destroy relationships. Maybe if we had stopped to think through those situations, the outcomes would have been more positive.

This section shows how our characters work through their respective situations.

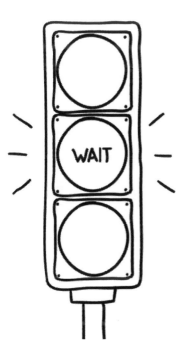

Chapter 10

ANNABEL

When we last looked at Annabel she was upset with her friend Kim for failing to honor their original plans. What was worse was that Kim hadn't thought to tell Annabel about the change in plans.

After getting off the phone Annabel sat on the couch. She was fuming. After five minutes of feeling sorry for herself and feeling just plain rejected she thought, "Ok...why am I so upset about this?"

A series of questions went through her head:

Is it because Kim treated our plans as though they weren't important?

Is it because she didn't call to inform me that the plans were off?

Is it because I just wanted to go out and have a fun time and couldn't?

The answer to all those questions was "Yes".

Then she thought about it from Kim's perspective:

Was she just so excited to spend time with her husband that she jumped at the opportunity?

Did she forget to call me because, in that moment, she genuinely forgot?

Could she have handled this with a little more courtesy?

The answer to all those questions was "Yes".

This step in the process is essential. Step outside yourself and look at the situation as an outsider. More often than not, peoples' actions are responses to their personal needs. We often perceive them as being selfish and inconsiderate, but if we start to recognize their behavior patterns and cues, it is so much easier to deal with them.

Once Annabel went through that process she concluded Kim had been careless rather than malicious. Annabel also gained insight into her own feelings and found that the disappointment of not being able to go out for a fun night was larger than any of Kim's mistakes. Disappointment is a direct result of unmet expectations.

Annabel felt calm at this point. She knew what type of actions were needed moving forward with Kim. She would talk to her the next day. Before that though, she would call a babysitter for next weekend so she could get some much needed alone time with her own husband.

Chapter 11

JOHN

After his interaction with Joe, John quietly walked back to his desk. His mind was still very active since he couldn't really understand why he hadn't been considered for a promotion. He sat down at his desk and stared blankly at the monitor for a minute. He knew he wouldn't be able to work given what had just happened. He had to clear his mind first.

John is going through internal confusion after his conversation with Joe; something many of us experience under difficult circumstances. "Waiting" and clearing his mind prevents him from executing any regretful actions.

John decided to go out to lunch. That way he could get himself out of the current environment and work through his thoughts more clearly. He took a notebook along with him so he could map out his decisions.

John drove out to his favorite restaurant and found a table in the corner. After giving his order, he pulled out his notebook and pen. He pondered for a minute how he would even go about doing an analysis. Then he realized he was so convinced he deserved the promotion that he hadn't considered why he *didn't* deserve the promotion. He knew it was going to be tough to figure out this aspect because confirmation bias is a roadblock for any type of problem-solving. In other words, he would need to be receptive to ideas and perspectives outside of his existing beliefs.

He decided to create a "WHY-WHY NOT" list. For a second he felt like Jim Halpert, a character from his favorite sitcom, who often resorted to a pros and cons list to drive a decision.

He started with the "Why" column and indiscriminately wrote down a few points. Then he came to the "Why Not" column. He sifted through his conversation with his boss and wrote down a few things. He then thought about what he could have done differently to influence the outcome and incorporated those things into the "Why not".

Looking at the last three items in the "Why Not" column showed him there were areas he could have done things differently. It was a lesson learned. He realized that every corporate journey would have learning moments such as this. Although he felt powerless in this situation, he knew he would need to make a few changes to really get the recognition he deserved. He felt calm enough to go back and have this conversation with his boss Joe.

John was able to work through his dilemma because he was willing to see if there was anything he could have done differently. Because of his openness, he was able to identify some things that were in his control that he could change.

Chapter 12

SARAH

After the heated interaction with her son, Sarah walked back to her room and sat down on her bed. Her heart rate was back to normal. She could hear nothing but silence.

She remembered the times when it was so much easier to be a parent. She recalled how time-outs and taking away privileges were so easy to execute when Kyle was a little boy. She realized those things had worked because she was in control and he just needed to abide by the rules. She paused at that point.

She wondered, "Is this about me needing to be in control? But isn't that my right as a parent?"

When we "expect" things to go according to *our* plan, we set ourselves up for disappointment. This also shows a lack of flexibility, making us less considerate. This rigidity directly influences how we respond when things don't go our way.

Sarah realized that she *did* want to be in full control. She always wanted things to be organized and predictable. That was how she ran her life, her career, and her home. That approach worked and it made her what she was today. She questioned why this situation with Kyle would be any different.

She wanted to list the "Worst Case Scenarios" of playing video games to share with Kyle. She thought it would help her justify her reaction to Kyle earlier.

She got out a piece of paper and started scribbling. Her final list looked like this:

Worst Case Scenarios (Of Playing Video Games)

- *Time Wasted*
- *Homework is not completed*
- *Potential Addiction*
- *Too much screen time*
- *Learning bad language*
- *Increased anger and frustration*

She looked at the list she created. She tried to solve the problem in her head. Although she had put time-restrictions around this before, she hadn't tied it to a "why". Since Kyle was a teenager now she knew it was time to adjust her approach in order to still be an effective parent. "Do it my way or the Highway" was not going to work anymore.

She had a plan and was ready to talk to Kyle.

Sarah's win in this situation was the mere fact that she was open to comprise. By being open to a two-way dialogue she was giving Kyle the recognition he needed as a teen - a person with an opinion of his own. Ultimately, we all want to raise our kids to make the right decisions. By guiding them instead of giving mandates, we as parents can help them work through those decisions. By explaining the consequences of their actions we encourage and empower them to, hopefully, make the right decision.

Chapter 13

JULIA

Swarmed with emotions, Julia sat at the dining table with her head buried in her palms. She had to take a few deep breaths just to get her heart rate and breathing back to normal. She knew her mind was spiraling out of control.

She recognized the disappointment she felt. She wasn't going to spend as much time with Josh as she had originally hoped. Then, she considered that Brandon might feel the same way about his time with Josh. She reflected on the fact that unlike Brandon, she gets to be with Josh every day. Would it have been better if Brandon's visit fell on a different day? Yes. Would it have been better if he had been on time? Yes. But that was not the case. There was nothing she could have done to prevent the situation. She could have told Josh not to meet Brandon at all by virtue of it being their anniversary. But that was really not who she was. She reminded herself she wasn't that unreasonable.

Here we can clearly see that Julia is a kind person and is considerate of others' feelings. Although she is disappointed initially, she quickly realizes that she should not take Josh's tardiness personally. Sometimes things happen unexpectedly.

She looked at the clock. It was seven-thirty. She was hungry. She thought she might actually be "Hangry". She figured Josh would probably not come home with the greatest appetite either. She turned on some music to relax before settling down to eat. She ate what she had prepared, but decided to save dessert. She wanted to share that with Josh.

Julia started feeling calm again. She realized she was wrong in doubting Josh's and Brandon's sense of reason. She was glad she hadn't gotten too carried away with creating a monster of the situation in her head.

She didn't feel like a "victim" after working through her feelings. She went on to enjoy and even savor her dinner with a sense of satisfaction.

Being able to adapt to change easily is a virtue that can be developed. Julia does it here by just "waiting" and acknowledging that things were really not as bad as they originally seemed.

SECTION 6
GO

Were you able to relate to the "WAIT" approaches of any of the characters? What is the style that would work best for you?

The hardest part about working through conflict is to think beyond yourself and your confirmation biases. The stories above show how each of the characters considered the other person's perspective to some extent.

That doesn't mean we all have to be saints and not care about our own needs. But it is about going beyond the "Why Me?" attitude. That would help us be less of a victim, less selfish, and less defensive. Recognizing that not everything is a personal dig is key in helping us be better and more balanced people.

This section shows us how our characters proceed on to the "GO" stage.

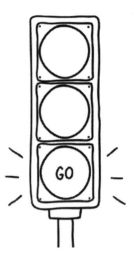

Chapter 14

ANNABEL

Annabel had worked through most of what got her upset with Kim. She had a certain level of clarity on what had happened. Her next step was to talk directly to Kim and address any remaining uncertainty or misunderstandings. This would be the best way to clear the air. It would teach Kim to be more self-aware and accountable for her own behavior in the future.

The next morning Annabel called Kim:

Annabel: Hey Kim! How are you?
Kim: Hey Annie - What's up? Hope you aren't mad at me for bailing on you.

Annabel paused for a second. She wanted to be honest, but did not want to come across as passive-aggressive.

Annabel: Well, that's what I wanted to talk to you about, actually.
Kim: Uh oh...am I in trouble?
Annabel: No. I just wanted to let you know that I understand how you may have lost track of our plans. I would jump at the chance to have a night out with my guy too. We all need non-mommy time.
Kim: Totally!
Annabel: Next time, if something comes up text me right away. That way I can re-adjust my expectations and maybe even make alternate plans.
Kim: Hey, sorry girl. I guess I sort of forgot in my excitement that you were counting on me.

Annabel: That's ok. I wanted to be open with you on how it affected me. I understand. A part of me might have even been jealous that you had a great night ahead and I didn't... at that point.

Kim: I get it. I was totally impulsive. That was selfish of me. I am so glad you told me. I'd rather have that than you being secretly mad at me.

Annabel: Yeah, I didn't want that either.

Kim: Thanks, Annabel. We can plan something for next weekend...maybe?

Annabel: Next weekend is date night. But I'll check my schedule and text you later?

Kim: Sounds good. Talk to you soon.

Annabel hung up the phone feeling totally at peace.

Chapter 15

JOHN

When John got back to the office he scheduled time to speak with Joe. He titled the meeting "Review Follow up". Joe was available the next morning.

John spent some time that night thinking about what his main talking points with Joe would be. He wanted the conversation to be to the point and effective and most importantly...emotion-free. He was hopeful that an objective conversation would help Joe understand and respect John's point of view.

The next day, John walked into Joe's office and shut the door.

John: Hey Joe. How are you?
Joe: Good, John. Is everything ok?
John: Yeah. I wanted to circle back on a few things we talked about yesterday.
Joe: Yeah? Ok. But I want to be clear - this is not going to change any decision that has already been made.
John: I understand that. In fact, that is what prompted me to set up this conversation.
Joe: Ok.
John: I wanted to be clear on my expectations going forward. I also wanted to make sure that we could be aligned on those things.
Joe: Certainly. What's on your mind?
John: I would like to walk through each of the goals we set this year and understand the reason for the rating. This will help me understand what was missing and how I can improve.

Joe: I appreciate that. You are the first one that has actually asked me to do that.

John: I know you recognize the quality of work I have been doing so I would like to have more assignments that touch a broader part of the organization.

Joe: Wow. That's a great ask. I can talk to my peers and see what I can do about it.

John felt like this meeting was going much better than the original one. He realized if he had taken a more proactive approach in the first place, it would have resulted in a more favorable outcome for him. He was hopeful this type of approach would bring him better satisfaction going forward.

John: Thanks, Joe.

Joe: Now then, let's take a look at the goal ratings.

Joe and John proceeded to review the goals. Joe provided a little more clarity on the ratings. John took notes on areas of improvement but wasn't afraid to share experiences that would contradict Joe's reasoning. John knew this was his opportunity to help Joe realize his contributions and maybe even see him as the budding leader he was.

After the discussion John thanked Joe for his openness and walked away feeling really content.

Chapter 16

SARAH

About an hour after Kyle stormed off to his room Sarah was calm enough to approach him.

She knocked on his door and slowly entered.

Sarah: Kyle?
Kyle: Yeah.
Sarah: I wanted to talk to you about what just happened.
Kyle: OK.
Sarah: I know I might have overreacted, but...
Kyle: Yeah you did.
Sarah: But I want to talk to you about why I reacted that way.

Sarah went on to explain the concerns she had laid out in her "Worst Case Scenario" list. She could see that Kyle was listening. When she was done, she waited to see how he would respond.

Kyle: Mom, don't you think I am responsible?

Sarah was a little dumbfounded by that question.

Kyle: I don't have a lot of homework this weekend. Also, my friends can't play later so we are playing now.
Sarah: Ok Kyle. But I still don't think you should spend hours playing video games. You can read, prepare for tests, or find other activities to do.
Kyle: Other activities...like what?

Sarah: Do your laundry or clean your room. These are all your responsibilities. They don't get done if you spend most of your time on video games.

Kyle: Mom!

Sarah: Ok, I get it. Let's come to an agreement. If you want to play for an hour in the afternoon and an hour in the evening that is fine. Before you do that, though, I need to know you have taken care of all your other responsibilities. Can we agree to that?

Kyle: Uh...maybe.

Sarah knew that was teenager code language for a hesitant "Sure..." She would take that for starters. She gave Kyle a hug and left his room feeling satisfied.

Chapter 17

JULIA

As Julia finished dinner she saw it was almost 8:00 PM and reached for her phone to check in on Josh. She took a deep breath and told herself she was not going to get mad if Josh was still with Brandon. She quickly made up a backup plan for a rain check in her head. She called Josh who picked up right away:

Josh: Hey Honey, I am about five minutes from home.
Julia: Oh. Did you leave earlier than expected?
Josh: Well, yeah. I knew you would be disappointed if we lost much more of the evening. I told Brandon I wouldn't be able to stay past eight o'clock because of our anniversary plans.
Julia: Really?
Josh: Yeah. He insisted we wrap it up by seven thirty.
Julia: Oh, that's sweet of him. We'll have to have him over the next time he is in town.
Josh: Yeah.
Julia: Ok. Drive safe. See you soon.
Josh: See you, babe.

Josh walked in the door about five minutes later. Julia gave him a bear hug. She didn't let go for a while. She felt so relaxed just being in his arms. She realized how much he meant to her.

"I love you babe. Happy Anniversary!" she declared. "Let's go have dinner...I have some cool news to share with you," she said with a coy smile. She was happy to start the celebration with Josh. She couldn't wait to tell him she was pregnant. She knew he would be ecstatic.

EPILOGUE

In all the stories above, the key to recovering from the situation was for each of them to purposefully "STOP". This allowed them to bring back the voice of reason and prevent over-reacting.

This is easier said than done, for sure! But the more this step is practiced, the less conscious we are about doing the work…it becomes second-nature. The duration of the "STOP" becomes shorter. Our bodies pick up the signal of distress and we know to rein in the chaos right away. We get to the point where our thought process becomes almost equivalent to a 4-Way Stop. There is a very short interval between observing and proceeding.

Once we slow down our thoughts, we think and behave more rationally. Relaxation and activities such as listening to music, taking a walk in nature and working out help us purge some of the wasteful thoughts in our head. Meditation is another tool that can be used to train our mind. It has been scientifically proven to help us clear our mind and slow down our thoughts.

The key is to be aware of ourselves, our surroundings and our thoughts in all situations. In other words, "Be Mindful".

We can also apply the same logic to our busy intersection scenario. There would be fewer accidents on the road if drivers/pedestrians paid more attention to the road. With the daily commute becoming an excuse for people to catch up with phone calls and texts, we are putting both ourselves and others at risk. Let's make that drive about being fully there and aware.

Enjoy the ride!

THE DOs and DON'Ts of STRESS MANAGEMENT

DO...

BE AWARE

Being aware of your body and mind at all times helps you recognize if something is going wrong. Any warning signs force you to take steps to resolve those symptoms. It is important to be present...in the moment.

PRACTICE

Patience and persistence are the key factors to success. Learning to control your actions takes time. It can seem like an impossible task at times, but the more you practice the three-step process outlined in this book, the easier it becomes.

MEDITATE

Take the time to clear and settle your mind. Choose whatever form of relaxation appeals to you. This gives you clarity and perspective and also helps you be more objective when faced with a difficult circumstance.

APPRECIATE

Learn to appreciate all the things that make you happy. Focusing on the positive aspects of life generally reduces the intensity of "negative" scenarios. This makes you stay calm in your response.

CELEBRATE

Every small achievement deserves a celebration. Acknowledge the progress you make along the way as you better yourself. Doing so encourages you to keep moving in the right direction.

REFLECT

Take the time to evaluate yourself and your actions. Taking this retrospective approach helps keep a finger on the pulse of areas that need attention. It also helps us recognize our strengths. Reflecting helps improve our integrity.

RADIATE

When you maintain a positive outlook on life you send out those vibes to the people around you. In the same vein, when you are around others that share this trait, you feel this energy. Being able to focus on the positives improves your chance for contentment.

SPEAK UP

It is important to provide your point of view in a calm and objective manner in times of conflict. Withholding your perspective only makes it more difficult to come to a resolution. By bottling up your feelings, you end up making a mountain out of a mole hill.

DON'T...

LABEL

The moment you put a negative "label" on someone you lose the ability to understand their point-of-view. When people are either insecure or frustrated, they tend to put on a facade of "power" so their vulnerabilities are not exposed. Take away the urge to label them, peel the onion a little to see if there could be something beyond the facade. This increases your compassion.

DWELL

Getting hung up on something bad that has happened to you in the past is not productive. Remembering and re-iterating such events simply compounds (and distorts) the effects of those memories. Letting go of the past encourages you to evaluate the status of the problem as it stands *today*. Doing that positions you to tackle any unresolved feelings or problems.

BLAME

Blaming others for your problems doesn't resolve anything. You have the power to make things better for yourself. Resist the urge to point the finger so you can view a problem more objectively. This will definitely yield more positive results.

REGRET

Everyone makes mistakes; some big, some small. The biggest mistake you can make is to wallow in the shame of that mistake. You are better off redirecting that energy into learning from that mistake to avoid making the same faux-pas in the future. Embrace more of a problem-solving mindset.

ASSUME

Sometimes you have to make decisions based on "assumptions". This makes sense when you don't have all the available information at that point in time. It does not, however, pay to make assumptions on people's intent or words. Confirmation bias can be a villain that prevents you from seeing someone's true intent. Evaluate every situation independently.

FRET

Worrying about matters is essentially a waste of time and energy. No amount of worry is going to fix a problem. This only makes you feel weak and helpless. You need to have the courage to stand up and deal with your problems head-on.

MAKE IT PERSONAL

Defensiveness is a response that people tend to use when their "pride" is attacked. If you were to take that "pride" out of the equation, you wouldn't be bothered by what people say about you. You could treat their comments as an opinion that you can choose to accept, or to deny. Taking out the personal angle makes you more willing to consider the other person's viewpoint and determine if it is valid or not.

ACKNOWLEDGEMENTS

This book has come to life thanks to a number of individuals.

My husband, son and daughter have encouraged me as a writer since my very first blog. They were even my in-home editors during this process.

My mom has always prayed for my well-being and success.

My family, friends, and colleagues cheered me on as I embarked on the final stages of getting this book ready.

The input from my editor, illustrator, book designer and formatter helped me achieve the simple and fun feel to this book without compromising its core messages.

Finally, my personal trainer. It was only after completing my first triathlon, with his guidance, that I realized my true potential.

Thank you.

STOP WAIT GO JOURNAL

You can use the following journal to capture your thoughts and feelings as you work through the STOP WAIT GO process in your life.

_____
_____
_____
_____
_____
_____
_____
_____
_____
_____
_____
_____
_____
_____
_____
_____
_____

82 STOP WAIT GO

STOP WAIT GO JOURNAL

86 STOP WAIT GO

Made in the USA
Middletown, DE
30 June 2024